Digital Marketing Mastery

Mastery

Skyrocket Your Business Online

Table of Contents

Chapter 1. Introduction

Unleash your business's full potential with the expert knowledge contained in our Special Report: "Digital Marketing Mastery: Skyrocket Your Business Online." Digital marketing is not a maze when you have a clear, marked path to follow — that's what our report offers. Even with zero technical knowledge, grasp the world of online marketing effortlessly as we walk you through its nuances in simple, easy-to-understand language. Whether you're a fresh startup, a seasoned small business, or a booming enterprise, our comprehensive guide will give you invaluable tools and insights to scale new heights. Let's explore the online hemisphere together and take your business to unprecedented levels of success. Get ready to transform your business journey with outcomes set to astound you - cheerful profits, expansion, and customer satisfaction like never before!

Chapter 2. Understanding the Digital Marketing Landscape

Understanding the digital marketing landscape requires a tour of its historical inception, growth, current situation, and future prospects. We'll start by exploring the evolution of digital marketing, the major components that comprise this space, and the role of technology in advancing the field. Through this comprehensive understanding, you'll be able to successfully navigate the digital marketing terrain and develop a personalized strategy.

2.1. The Evolution of Digital Marketing

In the late 1990s, digital marketing came into existence with the advent of the internet and the World Wide Web. Companies and marketers began exploring different avenues to connect with potential customers. Emails, banner ads, web directories, and search engine optimization (SEO) were among the early methods adopted.

Through the early 2000s, the internet population exploded, and by 2004, the advent of social media platforms like Facebook provided marketers with a completely new dimension for outreach. Google launched AdWords (now Google Ads), the pay-per-click service, revolutionizing online advertising.

The landscape further changed with the introduction of smartphones, quickly becoming the primary device for internet access. This led to mobile marketing initiatives such as in-app advertisements and SMS-based promotional campaigns. Today, with technologies such as Big Data, AI, and VR, marketers have unprecedented access to customer data and insights, making personalized and predictive marketing possible.

2.2. Major Components of the Digital Marketing Landscape

1. **Search Engine Optimization (SEO)**: This deals with improving your website's visibility on search engine result pages. It involves strategies like keyword optimization, quality content creation, and maintaining a user-friendly website design.

2. **Social Media Marketing (SMM)**: Leveraging social media platforms like Facebook, Twitter, LinkedIn, etc., to reach a wider audience, drive traffic to the website, enhance brand visibility and convert potential leads into customers.

3. **Content Marketing**: It involves creating and distributing valuable, relevant, and consistent content to attract and retain a clearly-defined audience. It can take the form of blogs, e-books, podcasts, newsletters, etc.

4. **Email Marketing**: It involves sending targeted promotional messages or newsletters to the subscribers. It helps in lead nurturing and maintaining customer relationships.

5. **Pay Per Click (PPC)**: Here, advertisers pay a certain fee every time their advertisement is clicked. It's a way to buy visits to your site rather than "earning" those visits organically.

6. **Affiliate Marketing**: It's a performance-based marketing tactic where you reward affiliates for every visitor or client brought through their marketing efforts.

7. **Mobile Marketing**: It involves marketing on or with a mobile device, such as a smartphone, through apps, SMS, MMS, social media, etc.

These major components can be used together or separately, depending on your business objectives and marketing budget.

2.3. The Role of Technology in Digital Marketing Evolution

Technology has played a major role in shaping the digital marketing landscape. Let's highlight three areas of technology that are currently defining the sector:

1. **Artificial Intelligence**: AI uses machine learning algorithms to analyze customer data and behavior to predict needs, automate tasks, and deliver personalized experiences.

2. **Big Data Analytics**: It allows businesses to gather, analyze and interpret large sets of data in real-time. This provides deeper insights into customer behaviors and trends that can be used to improve marketing strategies.

3. **Virtual and Augmented Reality (VR/AR)**: VR and AR offer immersive, interactive experiences that can increase user engagement and conversion rates.

As technology continues to evolve, so too will the digital marketing landscape. Keeping up-to-date with emerging trends and strategically incorporating these technologies can give you a competitive advantage in your market.

2.4. The Future Landscape

The future of digital marketing lies in personalization, automation, and an emphasis on providing value to the customer. To stay relevant, brands will need to adapt to the growing demands of omnichannel marketing, embracing a seamless user experience across multiple touchpoints.

Voice search, AI-driven customer service, chatbots, and predictive analytics are some of the technologies expected to dominate the future. IP targeting, programmatic advertising, and 5G-enabled ads will redefine the way businesses reach and engage with their audiences.

Also, ethics and data privacy will play significant roles. With regulations like GDPR in Europe, customers demand secure, transparent usage of their data.

To sum up, understanding the digital marketing landscape involves recognizing its dynamic nature. It has constantly evolved and will continue to do so. Therefore, studying its past, understanding its present, deploying the right technologies, and keeping an eye on future trends is vital to mastering the digital marketing game.

Chapter 3. Website Optimization: Making Your Online Home Inviting

Website optimization is your key to making your business's online home inviting. It is all about enhancing your website's aspects to improve its ability to drive traffic, engage visitors, and convert them into leads or customers. Simply put, an optimized website ensures the user experience is top-notch, thereby contributing to your business's overall success.

You will unravel the world of website optimization in this chapter, revealing some of the best and proven strategies you can follow to make your online home more inviting. We present these strategies in a simple and easy-to-understand language, so brace yourself for an informative and enlightening journey!

3.1. Principles of Website Optimization

Before making any changes to your website, it's essential to understand the fundamental principles of website optimization. These principles will guide your choices, helping you to create a website that satisfies your visitors and, ultimately, your business objectives.

1. User Experience (UX): A well-optimized website offers a smooth, pleasing, and intuitive experience to its visitors. Load time, navigation, and design all factor into the UX.

2. Accessibility: Your website should be accessible to everyone, including persons with disabilities. Employing accessibility features can dramatically increase your potential customer base.

3. Mobile Optimization: More people access the internet through mobile devices than desktop computers. It's critical your website is optimized for mobile use.

4. Security: An optimized website is a secure website. Users must trust your site, especially if it involves transactions.

3.2. Website Speed

Website speed is one of the first noticeable aspects of user experience. If your website takes too long to load, you'll likely lose visitors and potential customers. Here are some ways to improve your website speed:

1. Optimize Images: Large image files can slow your website. Use compression tools to reduce the file size of your images without sacrificing quality.

2. Minify CSS, JavaScript, and HTML: Minification removes unnecessary characters from your code, reducing the size of your website's files.

3. Use a Content Delivery Network (CDN): A CDN is a network of servers that deliver website content to users based on their geographical location. This reduces load time by serving the content from a server closer to the user.

4. Enable Browser Caching: Browser caching allows visitors' browsers to store copies of your website's pages. This dramatically reduces load time for returning visitors.

3.3. Mobile Optimization

As mentioned earlier, many people browse the internet using their smartphones. If your website is not optimized for mobile devices, you're potentially missing out on a substantial percentage of internet users. Implement these mobile optimization strategies:

1. Responsive Design: A responsive design ensures that your website adjusts to fit the screen dimensions of any device. This makes your website visually appealing and easy to navigate on smartphones, tablets, desktop computers, and more.

2. Legible Font Sizes: Make sure the font sizes on your website are large enough to read on small screens.

3. Touch-Friendly Buttons: On mobile devices, all actions are done using touch, not a mouse. Your buttons should be large enough for users to easily tap with their fingers.

3.4. Website Accessibility

By ensuring that everyone, including people with disabilities, can access your website, you make potential customers out of what's often an overlooked demographic. Here are some ways to make your website more accessible:

1. Use Alt Text for Images: Alt text describes the content of images to people who can't see them. It's read by screen-reading tools to help visually impaired users understand the content.

2. Provide Transcripts for Audio Content: People with hearing impairments will benefit from written transcripts of your audio content.

3. Avoid Automatic Navigation: If your website has slideshows or carousels, give users the ability to navigate them manually. Automatic navigation can disorient users with cognitive disabilities.

4. Use a Clear, Legible Font: Fancy fonts might look pretty, but they can be challenging to read, especially for people with visual impairments.

3.5. Website Security

Website security is paramount in inspiring trust from your users. With cyber threats on the rise, users are not keen on risking their data with unsecured websites. Bolster your website security with these strategies:

1. Install SSL Certificate: A Secure Sockets Layer (SSL) certificate encrypts data transferred between the user and your website. Websites with SSL have a prefix 'https' in their URLs, and browsers often display a padlock icon on such websites.

2. Regularly Update Website's Software: Keep all your website's software, including the content management system and plugins, up-to-date to guard against potential security vulnerabilities.

3. Use a Firewall: A good web application firewall (WAF) can block common threats such as SQL injection and cross-site scripting (XSS).

As you can see, website optimization is not a one-time thing but a continuous improvement process. It encompasses speed, security, mobile, and accessibility aspects. By optimizing these areas, your website becomes an inviting platform that offers a seamless user experience, engenders trust, and ultimately, drives conversions. Start implementing the strategies shared in this chapter, and watch your business grow online!

Chapter 4. SEO: Unlocking the Power of Search Engines

Every path to successful digital marketing begins with understanding the power of search engines. The term SEO, or Search Engine Optimization, might seem daunting initially, but it is, in fact, an uncomplicated concept that can propel your business towards staggering growth. SEO, in simple terms, is the art of making your business visible to potential customers through search engines like Google, Bing, and Yahoo. With an effective strategy, your website can rise to the top of search results — the coveted position that all businesses vie for.

This chapter will help you understand SEO and how to use its strategies to effectively direct traffic to your website.

4.1. Unlock the Basics: What is SEO and why does it matter?

People use search engines to seek information on virtually everything. Whether they need to buy a product, find a service, or learn something new, search engines are the go-to resource. Now, imagine the power of having your business at the top of those search results - your visibility to potential customers increases exponentially!

SEO is the technique of optimizing your website so that it ranks higher in search engine results, thereby bringing more traffic to your webpage and enhancing business opportunities.

If you're still wondering why it matters so much, consider these points:

1. It drives high-quality traffic to your website at no direct cost.

2. It enhances brand credibility. A high search engine ranking signifies trust.

3. It provides valuable insights into customer behavior and market trends.

4.2. Analyzing Keywords: The Foundation of SEO

Keywords are the cornerstone of SEO. They are the words and phrases potential customers type into search engines when searching for products, services, or information. Understanding the right keywords for your business is the key to crafting an effective SEO plan.

1. Conduct Keyword Research: Begin by brainstorming keywords related to your business, then use tools like Google Keyword Planner or Semrush to uncover more relevant keywords.

2. Analyze Search Intent: Understand what your potential customers are looking for when they use certain keywords.

3. Use Long-Tail Keywords: These are specific keyword phrases that are highly relevant to your business. They can be less competitive and often yield better results.

4.3. On-Page SEO: Optimizing for Success

On-Page SEO involves optimizing individual web pages for higher rankings and more relevant traffic. The focus here is on both the content and the HTML source code.

1. Optimize Your Title Tags: Include your keyword in the title tag.

It's one of the first things search engines (and users) see.

2. Use SEO-Friendly URLs: These should be straightforward and should include your keyword.

3. Use Headers: Break your content into readable and SEO-friendly chunks. Use headers (H1, H2, etc.) to highlight the main points.

4.4. Off-Page SEO: Boost Your Rankings

Off-Page SEO involves promotion techniques to improve the ranking of your web page in search results, focusing on factors outside your own website.

1. Backlinks: These are links from other websites to your site. The quality and number of backlinks are crucial ranking factors.

2. Social Signals: Social media can indirectly affect SEO. Shares, likes, and comments can help boost your site's visibility.

3. Guest Blogging: This can be an excellent way to secure quality backlinks and enhance your brand's visibility.

4.5. Local SEO: Connect with Your Local Audience

For businesses that operate on a local level, Local SEO is immensely beneficial. It involves optimizing your website to attract traffic from location-based searches.

1. Online Directories: Get listed in online business directories.

2. Google My Business: Create and optimize your Google My Business page for better local search visibility.

SEO might seem like a tough nut to crack, but with consistent effort and patience, you can significantly enhance your business's online presence. Always remember - good SEO translates to more visibility, increased lead generation, and higher ROI. Armed with the knowledge of how to unlock the power of search engines, steer your business towards the triumphant path of digital marketing success.

Chapter 5. Content Marketing: Crafting Your Brand's Story

Content marketing stands at the forefront of all digital marketing approaches — it's the sharpest blade in your marketing arsenal. A well-crafted content marketing strategy can help you refine your brand's voice, forge a deeper connection with your clients, and showcase the unique value your products provide. Yet, to turn content marketing into a formidable booster for your business, understanding its core elements, best practices, and nuances is quintessential.

Let's dive in and explore the world of content marketing, its mechanisms, its potency, and how you can exploit it to craft your brand's compelling narrative.

5.1. Understanding The Power of Storytelling

Narratives have a unique power to connect with people on a deeply emotional level. Since the dawn of civilization, humans have relied on stories to share knowledge, instill societal values, and form connections. Leveraging this inherent human tendency, businesses can create compelling narratives around their brand, thereby fostering deeper engagement with their audience.

In content marketing, storytelling transforms mere advertising into an immersive experience. It's not just about selling a product or service—it's about selling a feeling, an impression, a sense of affiliation to your clients. Therefore, it's vital to develop a well-defined brand story — one that consumers can relate to, which resonates with their ideals and values, gripping their emotions.

5.2. Crafting Your Brand's Story: Where to Start

First, you must understand your brand deeply. What does it represent? What values does it uphold? What's your mission? Who are your clients, and what do they value? These factors will help form the basis of your brand's story.

Creating a strong brand narrative requires an understanding of your customers' journey. You need to get into your consumers' shoes, feel their desires, their pain points, and how your product or service can solve them. That's paramount to create a compelling narrative that your consumers can associate with.

From here on, convey your brand story through myriad content types — web copy, eBooks, whitepapers, blogs, social media posts, videos. Your story should be consistent across all formats and platforms, enhancing audience experience and brand recall.

5.3. Key Elements of Content Marketing: Producing Effective Content

Effective content marketing is a delicate balancing act between providing value and entertainment. Your content should be both informative and engaging, providing solutions to your audience's queries, and leaving them wanting more.

Consider including client testimonies, real-life stories, behind-the-scenes narratives, in your content — deepening your audience's connection with your brand, and promoting trust. It's also crucial to use an authentic, consistent voice in your content, strengthening your brand image and identity.

Moreover, optimize your content for search engines. If your audience can't find you, the best stories won't work. So, utilize SEO effectively to improve the visibility of your content.

5.4. Amplifying Your Brand Story: Using Social Media

Social media platforms are indispensable tools for content marketing, helping amplify your brand's story. Tailor your narrative to fit each platform's content-distribution style and audience expectations. Embrace the medium's nuances—be it a tweet, a LinkedIn post, or an Instagram story—your content must speak the platform's 'language'.

5.5. Evaluating Success: Tracking Content Marketing Performance

To determine if your content marketing efforts are bearing fruit, you need to track your performance. Focus on metrics such as site traffic, conversion rates, SEO results, and social media engagement. Gaining insights on these will help you refine your strategy and improve future content.

Content marketing, when maximized effectively, will elevate your brand's visibility, foster audience connection, and bolster customer loyalty. That's the power of a well-crafted brand narrative. Understanding and leveraging these elements will put your business on a trajectory of growth, ever-reaching for the digital marketing stars. Cultivate your brand story, sing it from the virtual rooftops, make your brand not just seen, but felt. The journey is challenging, but victory is within reach. The digital realm awaits your compelling narrative. Get ready to witness the transformation!

Chapter 6. Social Media Strategy: Engage, Enlighten, Empower

Social media is a tremendous part of today's digital marketing landscape, offering you an invaluable avenue to engage with your customers, educate them about your brand, and empower them to become your brand advocates. Success in social media marketing is no overnight phenomenon. It requires a well-thought-out strategy, diligent execution, and constant engagement. To help you understand its vast potential and to effectively leverage the platforms, let's delve into the three crucial aspects: Engage, Enlighten, and Empower.

6.1. The Art of Engagement

Engagement is the heart of social media marketing. It entails creating content that appeals to your audience, capturing their attention and persuading them to interact with your brand. The engagement can take various forms: likes, shares, comments, or even direct messages for further information.

But how to create engaging content? First, you should understand your audience. Conduct thorough audience research to identify their interests, perceptions, and needs. They might be tech-savvy millennials looking for innovative solutions, or middle-aged professionals who value authentic connections; understand their demands.

Second, focus on creating content that resonates with your target audience, something you'd only know if you've conducted the above research correctly. Whether they're into edgy memes, expert advice, or personal anecdotes, it's your job to figure it out and deliver. Third, make sure to keep your posts fresh and consistent. Regular posting schedules help keep your audience engaged and familiarize them with your brand voice.

6.2. Enlighten: Education with Value

Once you've hooked your audience with engaging content, it's time to enlighten them. The aim is to educate your audience about your brand, products, or services in a way that creates value for them. Enlightening content can take the form of blog posts, how-to videos, infographics, or webinars.

Importantly, focus on demonstrating how your products meet their needs. Share success stories and customer testimonials. Collaborate with industry leaders for educational discussions. The key is to provide content that not only promotes your products but also offers helpful, relevant information for the audience.

Maintain a balance between promotional and informative content. Too many salesy posts will lead to audience fatigue, while too little promotion won't support your business goals. Aim for a healthy mix.

6.3. Empower: Inspiring Actions

Finally, it's time to empower your audience. Empowerment in this context means inspiring your audience to take action. Implicit in most marketing efforts, this type of content directs audiences to do something specific. Calls-to-action (CTAs) are an essential element here.

It might be a simple request to like or share your post, sign up for a webinar, download a whitepaper, or even purchase a product or service. The most effective CTAs are clear, compelling, and create a sense of immediacy. Slipping a CTA into your post or at the end can drive substantial conversions.

Beyond CTAs, another aspect of empowerment is cultivating a community. One of the greatest powers of social media lies in its ability to create and nurture digital communities. Encourage your followers to interact with you and with each other, building a brand community.

Remember, social media is not a one-way street. As much as it allows you to communicate with your audience, it also allows your audience to communicate with you. This reciprocal relationship is what sets social media apart from traditional marketing channels, and leverages its ability to foster brand loyalty and advocacy.

In conclusion, crafting a robust social media strategy is no simple feat, but with dedicated effort towards engaging content, educational value, and empowering actions, you can create a noticeable difference in your brand's online presence. Social media can truly be a game-changer for businesses willing to spend time understanding its intricacies and harnessing its potential wisely.

Chapter 7. Email Marketing: Reaching Inboxes with Impact

Email marketing has established itself as a key channel in digital marketing. It provides a personalized and cost-effective means to communicate with your customer base while giving you the reach and robust analysis capability of digital technologies. As such, understanding how to effectively utilize this tool is essential for any business wishing to improve their online profile and reach.

7.1. Understanding Email Marketing

Email marketing, at its essence, is as straightforward as it sounds: it's the use of email to promote products and services. However, it goes beyond its surface description. It enhances the relationship between a business and its customers, ensuring consistent and direct communication. When done right, it can help keep your customers informed about your latest offerings, encourage customer loyalty, and build a strong brand association in their minds.

7.2. Building an Email List

The backbone of successful email marketing is a well-built, well-maintained email list. This goes far beyond the act of just collecting as many email addresses as you can - the effectiveness of your email marketing campaign is directly related to the quality of your email list. Tailoring your list to include individuals who have shown interest in your business or industry improves your chances of turning a one-time visitor into a loyal customer.

To build an email list, start by adding a subscription form on your website and promote it across your social media platforms and other contact points with potential customers. Inform potential subscribers about what to expect in terms of content and frequency, and auto-responder technology can help you keep them engaged and loyal.

7.3. Crafting Effective Email Content

Creating impactful and engaging content is fundamental in any form of marketing, and email marketing is no exception. Depending on your company's offerings, content structure, tone, and language should be consistent and in sync with your brand's overall communication strategy.

To make your emails more engaging:

1. Use catchy subject lines. They're your first point of contact and can be the deciding factor for the recipient opening the email.

2. Always include a call-to-action. It should direct recipients towards your desired action, be it visiting your website, checking out a new product, or availing a discount.

3. Be personal. Use your customer's name and purchase preferences to make the email feel customized.

4. Keep it simple. Avoid jargon and complex words.

7.4. Understanding Email Analytics

Email marketing platforms provide rich analytical data about your emails. While these might seem complex at first, understanding the basics can go a long way in improving your campaign targeting and enhancing your returns.

Key metrics include open rates, click-through rates, bounce rates, and conversion rates. For instance, exceptionally high bounce rates may be an indication of irrelevant content, outdated email lists, or technical issues. Analyzing these figures and responding appropriately can make or break your email marketing efforts.

7.5. Embracing Automation

In this era where time is of the essence and personalization is key, automated email marketing campaigns can act as your secret weapon. With them, you can set off a chain of emails based on user actions or a set schedule. When implemented correctly, this can lead to better conversion rates and improved customer relationships due to the preciseness and relevance of these emails.

7.6. Adherence to Rules and Regulations

While formulating your email marketing strategy, it is essential to keep in mind the governing laws and regulations like the CAN-SPAM Act or GDPR in the European Union. Failure to comply can result in significant fines and reputational damage.

In conclusion, email marketing can be an incredibly effective tool when appropriately applied. By being proactive in building a high-quality email list, crafting engaging content, analysing success, embracing automation, and staying within the rules and regulations, your business can reach global inboxes with a substantial impact.

Chapter 8. PPC Advertising: Paid Promotions for Rapid Reach

Today's business landscape is more competitive than ever, and with the rise of the Internet, multinational companies, and globalization, the pressure to stand out and be heard has never been greater. However, with technologies like Pay Per Click (PPC) Advertising, getting your message across to your audience need not be an uphill task.

In the digital age, ignoring PPC advertising can be likened to leaving money on the table. This powerful form of online advertising offers instant visibility, competitiveness, and a more substantial ROI when harnessed correctly. So, let us dive right in to understand the more granularities of PPC Advertising.

8.1. Understanding PPC Advertising

Pay Per Click (PPC) advertising is a form of online advertising where advertisers pay each time a user clicks on one of their online ads. These ads could show up in search engine results like those from Google or Bing or on a host of partnered websites. The cost of these clicks is dictated by an auction-style bidding system, where keywords and audience characteristics are wagered for visibility. The allure of PPC advertising lies in its immediate results, control over budget, and its targeting capabilities.

8.2. The Mechanics of PPC Advertising

The first step towards successfully launching a PPC campaign is understanding its working. PPC advertising operates on a bidding system. Businesses bid on specific "keywords," which are terms or phrases users might use when searching for a product or a service online. For instance, if you're a shoe retailer, you might bid for keywords like "quality women's athletic shoes," or "best men's running shoes." When a user's search includes your keyword, your ad may appear in the sponsored results section of the search engine's results page.

But how do search engines decide which ads to place where? This is determined by the Ad Auction, an automated process that all major search engines run to determine the relevance and validity of the ads that appear on their search results pages.

8.3. Making the Most of the Ad Auction

Understanding how the Ad Auction works can offer you a strategic edge. Each advertiser sets a "Max CPC" — maximum cost per click they're willing to pay for a keyword. However, while this bid amount can affect where the ad is placed, it isn't the only factor. Search engines also consider the ad's relevance, click-through rate, and the landing page experience to decide the ad's ranking. This ensures even businesses with a smaller marketing budget can compete with larger corporations as long as they create high-quality ads.

8.4. Building a Successful PPC Campaign

Initiating a PPC campaign involves several tasks, each as crucial as the other. Right from doing keyword research to compiling those keywords into organized ad groups and ad campaigns, to setting up an optimized PPC landing page. Each of these steps plays an essential role in the campaign's overall success.

Keyword research is the foundation of a successful PPC campaign. But remember, exhaustive keyword research doesn't mean researching every possible keyword but finding keywords relevant to your business, have a large search volume, and exhibit an acceptable competition level.

When creating a PPC ad, your goal is to rank higher on the search engine results page (SERP). Higher ranking means better visibility and increased odds that potential customers will choose your business over your competitors. To help achieve this, you need to create compelling, well-written ads that offer clear, direct value to prospective customers.

The landing page should provide continuity from the ad and fulfill whatever promise was made in the ad copy. The same keywords the user searched should be found on this page to increase relevance and keep the visitor engaged.

8.5. Monitoring and Reporting

In digital marketing, every click, view, and action can be tracked, monitored, and evaluated. This ability to measure and quantify nearly everything makes PPC advertising a winner. With analytic tools, marketers can measure the number of impressions, clicks, and conversions made, to learn which ads are performing well and which are not.

8.6. PPC: A Viable Game Plan for Rapid Reach

In conclusion, when used effectively PPC campaigns can yield profitable results. However, like any digital marketing strategy, it requires consistent tracking, testing, and tweaking. Ignoring PPC in your digital marketing plan can mean missing out on potential clients and revenue. So, whether you're a small business looking for a way to get your brand out there or a large enterprise aiming to boost your online presence, a well-execified PPC campaign can be precisely what you were missing.

Remember, the journey of mastering PPC is a continuous process; there's always something new on the horizon. Keep learning, experimenting, and adapting your strategies to the ever-changing digital marketing landscape.

With the knowledge imparted through this chapter, we hope that you feel empowered to leverage the power of PPC Advertising to propel your business to reach new horizons. Good luck!

Chapter 9. Data Analysis: Interpreting Digital Performance

Getting to grips with the intricate world of data analysis is inevitably a substantial chunk of your digital marketing journey. To truly comprehend its significance, it's paramount to envision digital performance as a vehicle - it is already set and functioning, yes, but you as a driver have the privilege to influence its speed, trajectory, stability, and ultimately, the endpoint. That's exactly where data analysis fits in - interpreting digital performance to steer your business vehicle in the right direction.

9.1. Understanding Data Analysis

To break it down, data analysis involves scrutinizing, cleaning, remolding, and interpreting data to extract useful insights, draw conclusions, and aid informed decision-making. It is an essential practice in digital marketing, employed to gauge, optimize and steer a campaign's effectiveness.

Data, in its raw form, is merely an assortment of unsorted, unstructured info. It's through analysis that this info is transformed into meaningful insights. Think of it akin to a gold mining process - data collection is merely unearthing the ore, but it's the meticulous extraction process that brings out the invaluable gold - "insights."

9.2. Metrics to Focus on

As part of your data analysis, there are several metrics that can equip you with a deeper understanding of your performance online. These include:

- **Traffic**: The count of visitors to your website.

- **Channels**: The paths driving users to your website, e.g., direct traffic, referral, organic search, paid search, social, and others.

- **User behavior**: This entails metrics like bounce rate, pages per session, average session duration etc.

- **Conversions**: This includes any preferable action taken by a user on your website - making a purchase, subscribing to your service or newsletter, downloading resources etc.

9.3. Importance of Data Analysis

Understanding data analysis is quintessential for a myriad of reasons:

- **Identifying patterns**: With data analysis, you can identify patterns and trends in your web traffic, user behavior, and overall engagement.

- **Informing decisions**: A robust data-driven approach aids your decisions, serving as a reliable guide.

- **Setting realistic goals**: Evaluating previous and current performance paves the way for realistic, achievable goal-setting.

- **Optimizing results**: Based on analytical insights, you can optimize your marketing initiatives for better outcomes.

9.4. Implementing Data Analysis

You'll commonly employ platforms like Google Analytics for the implementation of your data analysis efforts. The transition from raw data to meaningful deductions involves several steps:

- **Data Collection**: This embodies gathering data from various sources like website traffic logs, social media analytics, online campaign metrics etc.

- **Data Processing**: This stage involves compiling the collected data to create a comprehensive data set.

- **Data Cleaning**: Here, you'll eliminate any errors, duplicates, or inconsistencies in the collected data.

- **Data Interpretation**: Finally, you'll interpret the cleaned data, using statistical analyses and machine learning algorithms to derive conclusions.

9.5. Putting Data to Work

Translating the derived insights into action is a decisive step. Depending on the deductions, modify your marketing strategy, optimize your website, refine your SEO techniques, or tweak social media campaigns. Remember, data is not just numbers. It reflects user behavior, buyer personas, preferences, patterns, allowing you to curate a more personalized, effective relationship with your audience.

9.6. Looking Forward

Interpreting digital performance through data analysis is a continuous endeavor. Remember, staying adaptive and flexible to the insights derived is key in this rapidly evolving digital landscape.

In conclusion, data analysis holds a crucial position in the domain of digital marketing. It's all about making sense of the numbers and using these insights to drive marketing decisions, user engagement, and ultimately, business growth. Understanding and implementing it prudently will indubitably set a firm, data-driven foundation for scaling your business heights. After all, when you measure, you grow!

Chapter 10. Online Reputation Management: Building Trust and Credibility

Credibility is the lifeblood of any business, more so in the digital world where trust is earned through various means. Let's delve into online reputation management (ORM), which is the process of monitoring and responding to online feedback about your brand, as well as proactively building a positive image.

10.1. The Importance of Online Reputation Management

In the digital age, a company's reputation could be built or shattered by a single online review, social media post, or viral news article. An impressive virtual image translates into brand loyalty and customer trust. Regularly monitoring your brand's digital footprint helps identify and mitigate issues before they escalate, increasing your credibility.

In essence, ORM is about fostering a positive brand image online. It involves prompt responses to negative feedback, enhancing online visibility, and the presentation of a convincingly positive image for your brand.

10.2. Understanding Your Digital Footprints

The first step in building a stellar online reputation is understanding your current digital footprint. It's essential to know what sort of online presence your brand already has. This may include:

1. Reviews on platforms like Google, Yelp, or Trustpilot.

2. Comments and mentions on social networks such as Facebook, Twitter, or LinkedIn.

3. Articles, blog posts, or other content mentioning your brand.

4. Forum discussions involving your products or services.

5. Any negative publicity or scandal that has been published online.

For a comprehensive analysis, consider using ORM tools like Google Alerts or social listening platforms. These will help track mentions and facilitate immediate responses.

10.3. The Art of Responding to Online Feedback

Once you understand your digital footprints, the next step involves how you manage them. This includes the ability to respond appropriately to both positive and negative feedback.

Commending positive feedback helps ensure consumer satisfaction and encourages brand loyalty. However, when faced with negative comments or reviews, your response can significantly impact how your brand is perceived. Here are some guidelines to help you navigate this sensitive area:

1. Address the reviewer politely and professionally.

2. Acknowledge their concerns.

3. Offer a solution where possible.

4. Apologize genuinely, if necessary.

5. Be proactive about rectifying the situation.

That said, never delete negative reviews or comments unless they violate policies. Transparency builds trust, and a well-handled negative review often generates more credibility than a score of positive ones.

10.4. Concrete Steps to Build Trust and Credibility

Beyond managing reviews, establishing a solid online reputation requires proactivity. Consider these steps:

1. **Quality and Consistent Content:** Regularly update your digital platforms with rich and relevant content. A blog can be an effective way to demonstrate your industry expertise, while social media posts can humanize your brand and bring consumers closer.

2. **Engage with Your Audience:** Engaging with your audience on social media platforms can help retain customers and attract potential ones. This can include promptly responding to comments, partaking in discussions, and even hosting competitions or giveaways.

3. **Be Transparent:** Transparency is key to building consumer trust. Ensure your business practices are clean and fair, and keep your customers informed about any changes or developments.

4. **Address Issues Promptly:** Promptly addressing issues shows your audience that you care for their satisfaction. This can be through providing refunds, replacing faulty products, or improving services based on feedback.

10.5. The Role of SEO in Online Reputation Management

Search engine optimization (SEO) also plays a crucial role in managing your online reputation. SEO strategies ensure your brand appears prominently in search results, outshining any negative publicity.

Keep your SEO up-to-date to ensure that prospective customers first encounter positive and useful information about your brand. With techniques like keyword optimization, backlinking, and producing high-quality content, your brand can achieve a dominant presence on the web, pushing ominous content into obscurity.

Online Reputation Management is an ongoing process, not a one-time fix. Keep refining your strategies continuously, taking in feedback, and elevating your brand reputation. Following the guidelines and steps provided above, you'll be well on your way to build a trustworthy and credible online presence for your business.

Chapter 11. Customer Retention Strategies: Nurturing Loyal Customers in the Digital Age

When it comes to growing your business, customer retention may hold the key. It's an age-old business saying - it's less expensive to retain existing customers than to acquire new ones. Now, let's take an in-depth look into the strategies for nurturing and keeping your loyal customers in the digital age.

Returning customers are worth your time and effort; they are the backbone that can champion your brand, referring you to their network, thus boosting your overall growth. Retention strategies in the digital age, unlike earlier times, are multi-pronged, focusing not only on customer satisfaction but also ensuring a memorable and personalized experience.

11.1. The Genesis of Customer Retention

Customer retention starts with understanding the customer lifecycle, which can be depicted in the following stages:

1. Discovery: The customer becomes aware of your products or services.

2. Consideration: The customer evaluates your offerings.

3. Purchase: The customer makes a purchase.

4. Post-purchase engagement: The customer interacts with your brand post-purchase.

5. Advocacy: The customer becomes a brand advocate and promotes your business.

Your role as a business owner doesn't end with the third step - Purchase. In order to retain customers, one must concentrate on mastering the final two stages, which are critically important for fostering a lasting relationship.

11.2. Crafting Memorable Customer Experiences

The digital age has amplified customer expectations. Navigating this labyrinth requires putting customer experience at the forefront. Here are some tools and strategies for crafting memorable customer experiences:

1. **Personalization**: Leverage customer data to provide personalized experiences. Use a CRM (Customer Relationship Management) software to develop strategies around your customers' behaviours, preferences, and needs.

2. **Quality Customer Service**: Exceptional customer service remains a key differentiator for businesses. Equip your customer service team with real-time access to customer data so that they can provide personalized support.

3. **Leveraging Technology**: Use technology to touch base with your customers often. Email campaigns, social media engagement, and mobile notifications keep your customers aware of your latest offerings.

11.3. Developing a Feedback Loop

A key part of any customer retention strategy involves capturing, analyzing, and acting on customer feedback. Use software tools to carry out regular customer surveys and act on the insights gained.

An effective feedback loop keeps your customers feeling valued and listened to, fostering loyalty.

11.4. The Role of Fostering Customer Communities

Building customer communities can serve as a platform for your customers to share their experiences and engage with your brand. This not only improves customer engagement but also turns customers into brand advocates.

With the right mix of strategies aimed at experiential excellence, data-driven personalization, regular engagement, feedback analysis, and community building, you can more effectively retain your existing customers.

11.5. Executing Retention Marketing Strategies

Retention marketing strategies target existing customers aiming to increase customer value over time. These strategies include:

1. **Loyalty Programs**: Reward your top customers with specials offers, discounts, or exclusive content.

2. **Re-engagement Campaigns**: Make use of email marketing or social media campaigns to rekindle the interest of slightly dormant customers.

3. **Upselling and Cross-Selling**: Suggest related products or premium versions of products that customers might find valuable.

11.6. Measuring Customer Retention

You can't manage what you can't measure. Understanding your customer retention rate is crucial to determining whether your retention strategies are working. Various software tools offer dashboards to track important metrics, providing insights into customer behaviour and the effectiveness of various strategies.

To conclude, in the digital age, although the means of retaining customers have changed, the core principles remain constant. The customer journey should deliver a memorable and satisfying experience from initial contact through to purchase and beyond. If executed well, customer retention strategies can transform your loyal customers into brand advocates, increasing the lifetime value of each customer and therefore, your overall business growth. If you build it right, they will not only come – they will keep coming back.